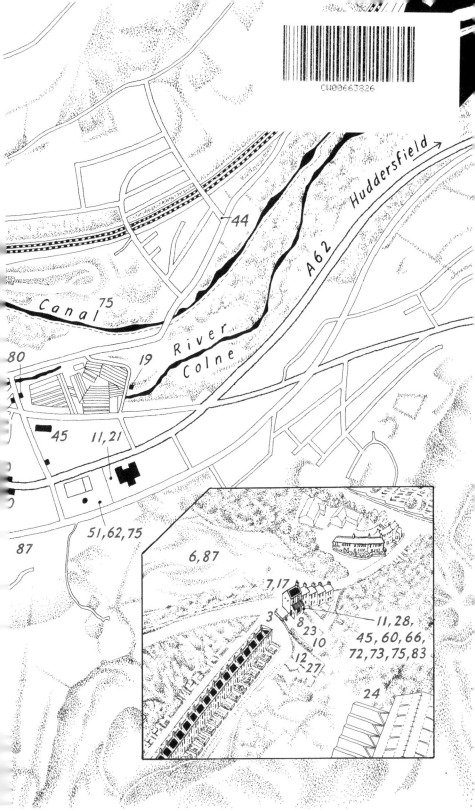

MAGNETIC FIELD

SIMON ARMITAGE

Magnetic Field

The Marsden Poems

ff

FABER & FABER

First published in 2020
by Faber & Faber Ltd
Bloomsbury House
74–77 Great Russell Street
London WC1B 3DA

Typeset by Typo•glyphix, Branston, Burton-on-Trent
Printed in the UK by TJ International Ltd, Padstow, Cornwall

A CIP record for this book is available from the British Library

ISBN 978-0-571-36144-1

The author gratefully acknowledges the publishers of
Human Geography (Smith/Doorstop Books, 1988) and
Zoom! (Bloodaxe Books, 1989), where some of these
poems first appeared

2 4 6 8 10 9 7 5 3 1

Contents

Introduction

Marsden is the last village in the Colne Valley as it climbs westward from the former textile town of Huddersfield into the West Yorkshire Pennines. The collar of moors and hills that surround it create a natural geographical amphitheatre. The settlement grew up at the confluence point of Wessenden Brook and the River Colne, with surrounding tributaries and gullies initiating a watercourse that eventually leads to the mouth of the Humber and flows into the North Sea. My parents lived in a terraced house on the south-facing side of Marsden (an end terrace, in fact, which we could claim as 'semi-detached' in more aspirant moments), up a steep, narrow road that was rumoured to be Roman in origin and still carries the contours of stone steps in the middle of the carriageway, beneath several layers of asphalt. My bedroom, made from a partitioned section of my parents' bedroom, looked straight down into the bowl of the village, the house occupying an enviable grandstand location for such a modest property. The only other terrace or 'block' with the same aspect consisted of twenty houses and was known colloquially as Titanic Row, either because of its impressive length, or because it was built in 1912, or because it was sinking slowly into the clay foundations. I watched a lot of TV as a kid and didn't read much other than comics, so I associate my first poetic experiences with the view from that bedroom window, especially the view at night, dreaming with my eyes wide open when I should have been asleep. I'd watch the streetlamps blink into action, the shutters and blinds go down in the shops at the top of Fall Lane, and headlamps illuminate distant lanes and gable ends. I'd watch people whose shapes and outlines

I recognised going into the New Inn or coming out of the Old New Inn, and curtains being drawn in the houses of neighbours and family friends. I'd see strangers, on foot or in unfamiliar vehicles, and I'd imagine incidents taking place behind closed doors, though none of this was ever written down at the time. It became a kind of compulsion, or at least a routine, thinking about the invisible goings-on, all the stand-offs and stalemates, the affairs and fisticuffs, the shenanigans and shady deals. Thinking also about the mundane and the commonplace, of people performing in the scenes and sketches of their regular lives, reinforcing my understanding of how the world worked and indulging a fascination with everyday domestic detail. Some of the excitement came from being completely inconspicuous, a secret and sly observer in an unknown lookout post, even when I watched my dad return home one night in his black tuxedo and white dress shirt and head off into the garden to water his tomatoes. These were private, moonstruck observations, like watching a clockwork model or staring into a diorama, but, in my peripheral vision, a dizzying and ominous blackness always loomed large. On those high uplands and across those wide moors there was literally no one, the truer proportion of Marsden's territory being a vast emptiness, full of terrifying and electrifying possibilities. At night, the horizon brimmed with a darkness like outer space, crowding the corner of the eye, thickening and deepening at the back of the mind.

Coming back to the village, after three years at Portsmouth Polytechnic, with no job, and in no hurry to get one, I started looking out of that window again, and out of the large picture window in the living room with its wide-angle view of Marsden – and I was ready to write. By that time I was a geography graduate with a head full of theories about people and places, a returning know-it-all with an eclectic education (geographer: 'jack of all trades, master of none'). So the village became the drawing board or board game on which I could practise my poetics and play out my perspectives. The frame of the window might have operated as a limiting device, restricting my perception of the wider world, but it was an invaluable template for bringing focus to the poems and legitimising the use of local subjects and vernacular in a poetic context. Maybe I was trying to fabricate some version of myself, forge an identity, fashion a sense of my situation in the universe, and the best materials – or only materials – to work with were those closest to hand. But if that's what I was up to, it was all taking place at a subconscious level. Back then I was just doing what came most naturally or conveniently and without a better option. So the post office got the treatment, as did the fire station, and the petrol station, and the snow-warning light on the main road. Even the house itself became a kind of 'cathedral of the ordinary' in that era of few material goods where possessions were somehow part of a ritualistic fabric of life and household events had a near-sacramental pattern and process. The slow succession of my dad's cars, for instance, became a way of recalling periods of family history: the Austin Princess era, the Datsun automatic years. Those vehicles, incomprehensibly expensive at the time, acquired the status of close relatives or large exotic pets, not just means of transportation but characters with names, personalities, idiosyncrasies and smells. Even though I'm pretty sure I never took a bite out of it I can still 'taste' the cracked red leather seats in the back of the Hillman Minx and picture the lettering on the registration plate: BAP 69P.

If all that goes some way towards explaining why I wrote

so much about Marsden in my first collection, *Zoom!* (1989), and my second collection *Kid* (1992), while I was still living there, it doesn't really explain why I've continued to address it – on and off – for another three decades. True, I only live a couple of valleys away, but in these parts that's the equivalent of self-imposed exile, and, since poetry became an unexpected passport, I've found myself travelling in all directions and towards all destinations. Yet distance seems to necessitate the occasional recalibration or rebalancing of the scales, as if I'm using the village as a standard of poetic measurement, or as a measurement of poetic standard. In 2015 I published *The Unaccompanied*, a collection that had accumulated slowly since around 2008, the year of the financial crash. Until I started to work out an order for the manuscript I hadn't realised how much I'd been writing about Marsden again, this time charting the effects of the recession, and the austerity that followed, and a growing sense of marginalisation in what was supposed to be an age of increased communication and connectedness. Not Goldsmith's *The Deserted Village* exactly, but some sort of fragmented twenty-first-century version of it. I'd also burrowed back into the past, perhaps looking for reassurance in the shape of prior experiences, but often finding those memories elusive, or unreliable, or ineffective bolsters against a volatile and unpredictable present day.

The village has changed. Many of the amenities and services I described in those early poems no longer exist. Two of the big mills are still standing, but are empty and decaying. New housing estates have replaced brownfield sites or encroached onto the moor. The moors themselves are greener and trees have sprung up even beyond the recognised 'tree line' – a consequence of climate change and reductions in chimney smoke and soot. And the giant eyesore of a gasometer, rising and falling like some grotesque iron lung, is no more. On the other hand, the basic layout is still the same, as is the population size, as is a sizeable proportion of the population. The infant and junior schools are still where they were. The football field – a prime central site – has resisted attempts to turn it into a low-budget supermarket. The clock on the Mechanics' Institute still pokes up above the rooftops on Peel Street, even if it rarely tells the right time. And Samuel Laycock, 'the Marsden poet' (what the hell do I have to do?), still looks out from his plinth near the bandstand in the park. So there's a surface continuity, at least, to draw on and return to, as well as a continuity of vocabulary and dialect. These days a 'regional accent' is usually thought of as a marker of authenticity and identity, but growing up we were told to speak 'properly' and sometimes threatened with elocution lessons, because with the unsophisticated noises that came out of our mouths we would never get anywhere.

Beyond the linguistics, I've come to feel that there is something genuinely unique about Marsden as a liminal, transcendent and transgressive location: a border area where habitation meets the uninhabitable; where Yorkshire meets Lancashire (not just topographically, but culturally); where the land disappears into the sky on many days of the year; where the last lawn is separated from the moor by the dividing line of a privet hedge; where absentee aristocratic landowners meet (or rather don't meet) tenants, hill farmers and ramblers; and where roads peter out into cart-tracks and bridleways. The residents who have resurrected pagan fire festivals in Marsden and celebrate the zeal and resistance of the local Luddites chapter are the same people waiting at the station in the morning, commuting to IT jobs in Manchester and Leeds. The village was an extraordinary adventure playground for a child, with its system of switchbacks, towpaths and unadopted roads, and with its many reservoirs, like a sleeping pantheon of water deities above our heads, whose names became a recited litany of localness and belonging among those in the know. More recently they have lent their titles to beers in the village brewpub, though I've never found a pint of Butterley or Cupwith an especially refreshing thought, remembering some of the things we found in those bodies of water, and some of the things we did in them. In attempting to describe border regions as good places to write – for the friction and exchange that takes place along the collision front – I once said in an interview that I grew up with one foot on the pavement and the other in the pigsty, something of an exaggerated claim (in fact, on Old Mount Road there were neither). But on Pule Hill, the landmark above Marsden with its distinctive silhouette, prehistoric burial sites and caves exist side by side with quarries and ventilation shafts from the railway tunnel beneath, more honest indicators of the kind of duality or interface I was trying to articulate. My poem 'Snow' is carved into the rocky escarpment on the exposed flank of Pule Hill, the first of six Stanza Stones that form a fifty-mile trail from Marsden to the far side of Ilkley Moor. Thus far it's the only one to be vandalised. Just bored kids throwing rocks, probably, but a useful caution against being a priest in your own parish. I've assigned Pule Hill many designations in the past – homing beacon, trig point, watchtower – though in the context of this collection and its given title, it is as a lodestone or magnetic pole that I'm now thinking of it.

A few years ago my parents reluctantly flitted from the house they had lived in for over half a century to a house in the village centre, a property near a bus stop, shops, the church, pubs, the doctors' surgery, and somewhere that doesn't require a gritting lorry and grappling irons to make it accessible when one of those old-fashioned winters rolls in. The reluctance was mine, too; having identified the house I grew up in as a kind of creative wellspring, it crossed my mind that without it I might dry up. If anything, though, not having a foothold in that property, and having emptied it of family possessions, I've felt able to investigate it more freely and without the obligations that superstition and nostalgia can sometimes impose. Free to be more honest, and free to mythologise.

A few years ago a producer and presenter from BBC Radio 4 invited me to read some of my Marsden poems *in situ*. So a local builder let us into the boarded-up fire station and I read 'Emergency' as we crunched around on the broken glass on the floor. Then I read 'Harmonium' in St Bartholomew's Church, and 'Leaves on the Line' at the railway station, and 'On Marsden Moor' on Marsden Moor. Finally we pulled up outside the old house, and, sitting on a wall across the road, I was just about to read 'Kitchen Window', or 'Privet', or 'Camera Obscura', or 'Miniatures', or 'Greenhouse', or 'After the Hurricane', or several others located at the same address, when the new occupier emerged from the back door with a large hammer and started to unceremoniously demolish my dad's rose arch, the one he'd cobbled together with lengths of Tanalised 4 × 2 and long rusty nails. It wasn't the prettiest of structures, but it had withstood many meteorological assaults. Watching it buckle and collapse with just a few blows should have wrong-footed me, but those who listened closely to the broadcast will have heard suppressed giggling in the background – the involuntary response to an incident that was too good to be true from a programme-making point of view and too obviously poetic for a poem.

This edition gathers together fifty of my Marsden poems. I have attempted to order them chronologically – not by the dates they were composed or first published, but by the dates they describe. It was an impossible timescale for all kinds of reasons: some of the poems don't relate to any particular day, month or year, while others refer to several. But to my eye and ear, at least, situating the poems alongside different neighbours and releasing them from the sequence of their construction has given them new resonances, just as the maps that bookend this collection return them to their original geographical locations (the numbers on the maps refer to page numbers in the table of contents), situating the poems in space rather than time. I have included one poem from my first ever pamphlet, *Human Geography* (1988), which didn't make the transition to the adult world of mainstream publishing back in the day but seemed worthy of a recall in this context. And I have added a handful of new poems, from an ongoing future collection, to show how the village continues to exert its influence and the attraction shows no signs of fading.

SIMON ARMITAGE
2019

MAGNETIC FIELD

Miniatures

A washing line strung between our house and theirs,
those neighbourly neighbours, settlers
from a lost age and a childless planet.

    In this flashback scene
I'm the kid sprawled on their front-room carpet
       staging shows and plays
with the sugar-glazed Capodimonte pieces
in the opera house of their hearth and fireplace:

the reclining shepherd, the snooty princess,
the drunken soldier, the tramp on the bench,
       the pig in the trough
       and the rearing horse,
every figure worth a fortnight's wages.

          *

Teaspoon. Tack. Spokeshave. Bit.
Thimble. Bradawl. Crochet hook.

          *

For my twenty-first I hunted down
a first edition of George Mackay Brown's
       Fishermen with Ploughs
with the netted shoal and plough at rest
       on the brick-coloured cover,
       and handed it over.

Then they handed it back, gift-wrapped
in waxy brown paper and gardening twine
with a fiver, like a bookmark, slipped inside.

*

The apple seller.
A wren in its nest.
The poised ballerina.
The scribe at his desk.

*

When I lift the lid of the model village
they're just as I left them, tinkering, grafting.

The king in his kingdom
of hen-scratched earth, a soft flurry
of Rhode Island Reds around his work-boots,
or alone in the shed among oil-guns and ratchets,
        hunched and wordless.

The queen in the gathered light of the porch
        knotting coasters, doilies,
cushion covers and christening bonnets
with a worn tortoiseshell tatting shuttle
        and fish-eye needles.
Or through veils of steam, glistening and ghostly,
rising from the cellar draped in laundry,
        the yard a surrender
of boil-washed sheets and pillow cases.
        I see white paper, clean pages.

Camera Obscura

This eight-year-old sitting in Bramhall's field,
shoes scuffed from kicking a stone,
too young for a key but old enough now
to walk the short mile back from school.

He's spied his mother down in the village
crossing the street, purse in her fist.
In her other hand her shopping bag nurses
four ugly potatoes caked in mud,

a boiling of peas, rags of meat or a tail of fish
in greaseproof paper, the price totted up
in pencilled columns of shillings and pence.
How warm must she be in that winter coat?

On Old Mount Road the nearer she gets
the smaller she shrinks, till he reaches out
to carry her home on the flat of his hand
or his fingertip, and she doesn't exist.

~

the kitchen window
        distraught with steam,
                my mother at the twin-tub

manhandling shirts,
        hauling drowning sailors
                from sea to deck

Orion

Ten or eleven, back-packing in the front garden. Summer,
its back broken. An air-rifle, .22, spring-loaded, snapped
open. A bullet-belt and a combat jacket, me tracking
big game through papery brown scrolls of dead bracken.

Broken glass underfoot spiking a vein in the ankle
under the knuckle of bone. Later, bandaged up,
unwrapping a pin-prick of blood to a full-blown rose,
red blooming out through the coils of the strapping.

The Chisel

You and him, a two-man chain-gang, making sparks
    by shaping
millstone grit to raise a wall. When split, each rock
lets fly its smithereen of heat, except this stepping-stone
of ganister, a cubit long each side, that will not give.

You hold the chisel in a double-handed fist. He lifts
the hammer up above the ridges and the peaks,
    brings home
the height of Puddle Hill, Scout Head, Pole Moor,
    West Nab,
onto the nub of steel, into the metal nib.

The Shout

We went out
into the schoolyard together, me and the boy
whose name and face

I don't remember. We were testing the range
of the human voice:
he had to shout for all he was worth,

I had to raise an arm
from across the divide to signal back
that the sound had carried.

He called from over the park – I lifted an arm.
Out of bounds,
he yelled from the end of the road,

from the foot of the hill,
from beyond the lookout post of Fretwell's Farm –
I lifted an arm.

He vanished from sight, went on to be twenty years dead
with a gunshot hole
in the roof of his mouth, in Western Australia.

Boy with the name and face I don't remember,
you can stop shouting now, I can still hear you.

Privet

Because I'd done wrong I was sent to hell,
down black steps to the airless tombs
of mothballed contraptions and broken tools.
Piled on a shelf every daffodil bulb
was an animal skull or shrunken head,
every drawer a seed tray of mildew and rust.
In its alcove shrine a bottle of meths
stood corked and purple like a pickled saint.
I inched ahead, pushed the door of the furthest crypt
where starlight broke in through shuttered vents
and there were the shears, balanced on two nails,
hanging cruciform on the whitewashed wall.

And because I'd done wrong I was sent
to the end of the garden to cut the hedge,
that dividing line between moor and lawn
gone haywire that summer, all stem and stalk
where there should have been contour and form.
The shears were a crude beast, lumpen, pre-war,
rolling-pin handles on Viking swords,
an oiled rivet that rolled like a slow eye,
jaws that opened to the tips of its wings
then closed with an executioner's lisp.
I snipped and prodded at first, pecked at strands,
then cropped and hacked, watching spiders scuttle
for tunnels and bolt-holes of woven silk,
and found further in an abandoned nest
like a begging bowl or a pauper's wreath,
till two hours later the hedge stood scalped
and fleeced, raw-looking, stripped of its green,

my hands blistered, my feet in a litter
of broken arrows and arrowhead leaves.

He came from the house to inspect the work,
didn't speak, ran his eye over the levelled crown
and shorn flanks. Then for no reason except
for the sense that comes from doing a thing
for its own sake, he lifted me up in his arms
and laid me down on the top of the hedge,
just lowered me onto that bed of twigs,
and I floated there, cushioned and buoyed
by a million matchwood fingertips,
held by nothing but needling spokes and spikes,
released to the universe, buried in sky.

Capricornus

On my first visit to the Yorkshire Avalanche Dodgers,
they brought in a shaggy old goat by its handlebars,
which was Ronald Dyson's, or it was Ronald Hodge's.
I was thinking of knives and blood, but it opened its arse

and the president counted its turds as a kind of raffle.
There were thirty-one, as it happened, excluding
globular clusters, nebulous objects and other dark matter.
The goat breathed in through its horns as Harry Ronson

sent his hand in search of his missing five-pound note
as far as his elbow into the sleeve of the animal's throat.
On a later visit, we ate chicken served from a
    shopping basket
and thick-cut chips passed round in a bucket.

Twist

The spotlight threw its custard pie and missed.
A wench in a bodice sold fancy sweets;

slung from her neck, the tray of Walnut Whips
stood in the shadow of her powdered breasts.

The Widow Corney, sherry on her breath,
popped Tic-Tacs in the wings. The chorus line

smoked musky roll-ups on the fire escape.
A mutt with stage fright, Bullseye flinched and pissed

when Bill Sykes raised his stick to Nancy's face.
Three make-up ladies dusted Fagin's schnoz,

unreconstructed and pre-Holocaust.
His cutpurse gang were roughnecks in real life:

between dress rehearsal and opening night
the Artful Dodger had pointed his knife

at Oliver's voice – unbroken and choice –
asked if his balls had dropped, fucked with his head

till the Adam's apple in pretty boy's throat –
quavering, ripe – hung by a slender thread.

Kitchen Window

You wanted more view, more day. So out
came the heavy sashes and bevelled frames,
the dulled soft-focus cataracts of old glass,
and the counterweights – dumbbells of crude iron
hanging on frayed ropes – all thrown in the skip.

Wrapped in a canvas sheet the brand new pane
rode on the side-rack of the joiner's van.
Undressed and carried, cloudscapes tilted
in its mirror and the planet swayed, though
set in place it seemed a solid nothingness –
a panel of air or frozen light
that magnified its own transparency.

Simian, almost, in nature and name,
I could swing up onto the outside ledge
and hunch in the angle of wall and lintel,
my ankle hooking a plastic bucket half-filled
with a lukewarm broth of bloated sponges and cloths
and a slimy liver of chamois leather
for swabbing the glaze.

                              From inside the house
the hummingbird of your hand and finger
pointed or tapped at streaks and smears, or your face
came close to the brink to mouth instructions
then fell away behind net curtains.
Then fell away further, sinking to deeper
darker reaches and would not surface.

A New Career in a New Town

David Bowie called. Before I could get into the specifics of him being dead and this being a private, unlisted number, he said, 'That's a foreign ring-tone, man – are you abroad? Always had you pegged as a bit of a stop-at-home, curled up in your Yorkshire foxhole.' I told him I was in Ysp, flirting with communism, alienation and Class A narcotics, and working on my experimental Ysp trilogy. He said, 'Simon, your imagination is telling lies in the witness box of your heart. But listen, will you write the lyrics for my next album?' 'Why not,' I replied, and quickly we thrashed out a plan of action. It would all be done by electronic communication – no personal contact, no face-to-face meetings. David *laid down some backing tracks* and over the next year or so I worked up a suite of songs – verse-chorus stuff, nothing too pretentious or avant-garde. 'These are genius, man. You could have been a poet!' he said, laughing like a cheeky cockney in the saloon bar of a south London boozer circa 1969, his voice like cigarette smoke blowing through a pre-loved clarinet. 'One thing I always wanted to tell you, David,' I said. 'When I was about thirteen I was really into table tennis but had no one to play with. It was just me versus the living room wall, on the dining room table. One night I went down to the local youth club, where all the roughnecks used to hang around, and made my way to the top floor where the roughnecks were playing table tennis, lads who'd stolen cars and thrown punches at officers of the law. I was wearing shorts and sweatbands in the style of my favourite Scandinavian table tennis champion of the era whose deceptive looping serve I hoped one day to emulate and whose life I wanted to live. I felt like a kid goat pushed into the tiger enclosure at feeding time, but they ignored me, those roughnecks with their borstal-spot tattoos and broken teeth, just carried on playing, the small hard electron of the ball pinging back and forth across the net like the white dot in that seventies video game.' 'Pong,' said David. 'Exactly,' I said, 'Just carried on smoking and swearing and hammering the ball to and fro under the yellow thatch of the canopied light in the darkened upstairs room. And here's the thing: every time he hit a winner, the roughest of those roughnecks would sing a line from *Sound and Vision*. 'Blue, blue, electric blue, that's the colour of my room,' he'd croon as he crashed a forehand to the far corner of the table, or 'Pale blinds drawn all day,' when he flipped a cheeky backhand top-spinner past his bamboozled opponent. You probably scribbled those words on a coaster in a Berlin cocktail bar or doodled them with eye-liner pencil on a groupie's buttock, but they'd carried all the way to a dingy youth club in a disused mill under a soggy moor, into the mouth of one of those roughnecks, who's probably dead now or serving life.' David sounded pensive on the other end of the phone, perhaps even a little tearful. 'I have to go now,' he said. I could hear the technician checking his seatbelt and oxygen line for the last time, touching up his mascara, lowering his visor. Then the engines started to blast and the countdown began. I wandered down to the big Henry Moore in the park and lay on my back in the crook of its cold bronze curve, watching the skies, waiting for the crematorium of night to open its vast doors and the congregation of stars to take their places and the ceremony to begin.

The Tyre

Just how it came to rest where it rested,
miles out, miles from the last farmhouse even,
was a fair question. Dropped by hurricane
or aeroplane perhaps for some reason,
put down as a cairn or marker, then lost.
Tractor-size, six or seven feet across,
it was sloughed, unconscious, warm to the touch,
its gashed, rhinoceros, sea-lion skin
nursing a gallon of rain in its gut.
Lashed to the planet with grasses and roots,
it had to be cut. Stood up it was drunk
or slugged, wanted nothing more than to slump,
to spiral back to its circle of sleep,
dream another year in its nest of peat.
We bullied it over the moor, drove it,
pushed from the back or turned it from the side,
unspooling a thread in the shape and form
of its tread, in its length and in its line,
rolled its weight through broken walls, felt the shock
when it met with stones, guided its sleepwalk
down to meadows, fields, onto level ground.
There and then we were one connected thing,
five of us, all hands steering a tall ship
or one hand fingering a coin or ring.

Once on the road it picked up pace, freewheeled,
then moved up through the gears, and wouldn't give
to shoulder-charges, kicks; resisted force
until to tangle with it would have been
to test bone against engine or machine,
to be dragged in, broken, thrown out again

minus a limb. So we let the thing go,
leaning into the bends and corners,
balanced and centred, riding the camber,
carried away with its own momentum.
We pictured an incident up ahead:
life carved open, gardens in half, parted,
a man on a motorbike taken down,
a phone-box upended, children erased,
police and an ambulance in attendance,
scuff-marks and the smell of burning rubber,
the tyre itself embedded in a house
or lying in the gutter, playing dead.
But down in the village the tyre was gone,
and not just gone but unseen and unheard of,
not curled like a cat in the graveyard, not
cornered in the playground like a reptile,
or found and kept like a giant fossil.
Not there or anywhere. No trace. Thin air.

Being more in tune with the feel of things
than science and facts, we knew that the tyre
had travelled too fast for its size and mass,
and broken through some barrier of speed,
outrun the act of being driven, steered,
and at that moment gone beyond itself
towards some other sphere, and disappeared.

Greenhouse

It's gone to seed now; each loose pane pitted
with lichen like the walls of a fish tank,
the soffits lagged with a fur of cobwebs.
I burst in the other day; kicked the door
out of its warped frame, stood in the green light
among nine years of unnatural growth
and thought back to the morning we built it.
We used the old sash windows from the house,
held them flat with leather gloves, steadied them
down the path. I remember that journey:
you out in front, unsure of your footing
on the damp stones, and me behind counting
each of your steps through our cargo of glass.

Some nights I'd watch from my bedroom window
as you arrived home late from a concert,
and leaving the headlights on to guide you
waded into the black of the garden.
I'd wait, straining for the sound of the hasp
or guessing your distance by the sparkle
of a cufflink. When you disturbed them
the seeds of rose-bay willow-herbs lifted
like air bubbles into the beam of light.
Then you'd emerge, a hoard of tomatoes
swelling the lap of your luminous shirt;
and caught in the blur of double glazing
your perfect ghost, just one step behind you.

Without Photographs

We literally stumble over the bits
and pieces, covered with ash
and tarpaulin, stashed into corners,
all that tackle under the old mill.
I don't know how we finally figure it out,
poking around in the half-dark,
coming across the neatly coiled strips
of soft lead flashing
and the fire-blackened melting equipment,
but it all fits together, falls into place.
For three weeks we light up the adapted oil-drum
with anything combustible:
door frames from the tip, spools, bobbins,
pallets, planks, old comics even which we sneak
from the house beneath our anoraks
and deliver on the run like parachute drops.

When we are forced to take a few steps backwards
and the heat stays in our faces like sunburn –
that's when the fire is hot enough.
We slide the melting-pot across the grill
(a stewing pan with no handle, a cooker shelf)
and toss in the lumps of lead
like fat for frying with. It doesn't melt
like butter, slowly, from the bottom upwards
but reaches a point where it gives up its form
the way the sun comes
strongly around the edge of a cloud.
Then it runs, follows the dints
in the pan, covers the base so we see ourselves –

an old mirror with patches of the back missing.
For moulds we use bricks.
Like stretcher-bearers we lift the pan
between two sticks then pour the fizzing lead
into the well of a brick.
Sometimes it splits it clean in half with the heat.

Today we watch the mould, prod it
through its various stages of setting, and can't wait
to turn it out like a cake, feel
its warm weight and read the brickwork's name
cast in mirror writing along its length.
But in the days that come, the shapes will mean less
and less, giving in to the satisfaction of the work.
What there is in the sweat, and the burns,
and the blisters, is unmistakably
everlasting. Not what is struck in the forged metal
but in the trouble we know we are taking.

And something about friends, walking home,
grinning like bandits, every pocket
loaded,
all of us black-bright and stinking like kippers.

The Serpent-Holder

Someone local swiping eggs at night
from Redfearn's creosoted chicken coop.
Redfearn kipping in the hutch two weeks
until an arm slides through the hatch.

Redfearn: *Got thee, bastard.* Egg-thief:
Happen, but tha dunt know who I bastard am.
Fair point. Ten minutes' Chinese burn, then pax,
then egg-thief legs it after shaking hands.

True North

Hitching home for the first time, the last leg
being a bummed ride in a cold guard's van
through the unmanned stations to a platform
iced with snow. It's not much to crow about,

the trip from one term at Portsmouth Poly,
all that Falklands business still to come. From there
the village looked stopped; a clutch of houses
in a toy snow-storm with the dust settled

and me ready to stir it, loaded up
with a haul of new facts, half expecting
flags or bunting, a ticker-tape welcome,
a fanfare or a civic reception.

In the Old New Inn two men sat locked
in an arm-wrestle – their one combined fist
dithered like a compass needle. Later,
after Easter, they would ask me outside

for saying Malvinas in the wrong place
at the wrong time, but that night was Christmas
and the drinks were on them. Christmas! At home
I hosted a new game: stretch a tissue

like a snare drum over a brandy glass,
put a penny on, spark up, then take turns
to dimp burning cigs through the diaphragm
before the tissue gives, the penny drops.

As the guests yawned their heads off I lectured
about wolves: how they mass on the shoreline
of Bothnia, wait for the weather, then
make the crossing when the Gulf heals over.

Somewhere Along the Line

You met me to apologise, you were saying
as we waited in the drizzle for the slow train.
When it focused in we said goodbye and we kissed
and from the window you were caught; teary and fixed.

You ran across the wooden bridge, I knew you would,
to get down on the other platform and to wave,
but as you did the eastbound Leeds train flickered past
and ran you like a movie through its window-frames.

I keep those animated moments of you as
our catalogue of chances rushed and chances missed.

Don't Blink

Because the six-year-old on the pavilion steps
keeps stepping out of her mother's sling-back sandals
and a jogger on the road has barely enough breath
to say 'It never gets any easier, just quicker'
to his brother who is hoisting a double baby-buggy

over the narrow gate. Other things we can take
or leave: the ambulance that stubs its shock absorbers
on the sleeping policeman; the incensed batsman walking
back towards the bowler, saying if he does that again
he'll ram this steel-sprung Duncan Fearnley down his throat

or through the windscreen of his Ford Fiesta.
Not that this match could be close or anything;
the home team only have nine men and one of those
is the scorer's friend, who at a sensitive age looks
ridiculous in blue shorts and his sister's jumper.

Don't blink. You might miss the perfect smile
of a boy whistling 'Summertime' who has to stop
when he gets to the bit that goes 'Your daddy's rich'
or the man with a dog who turns to ask his friend
why they can't make aeroplanes out of the same stuff

they make black-box flight recorders out of.
You might not even notice that an evening breeze
which wafts the drone of a moorland rescue helicopter
across the field from a mile away, is the same breeze
that chafes the tip from a pile of sawdust

and rocks the jumper of the left-arm spinner, mislaid
for the moment, on the handle of the heavy roller.
The fight in the beer tent hardly gets a mention.
When the light fades, the swifts say more about the weather
than a poet ever could, picking up the smallest insects

dangerously close to the ground.

The Catch

Forget
the long, smouldering
afternoon. It is

this moment
when the ball scoots
off the edge

of the bat; upwards,
backwards, falling
seemingly

beyond him
yet he reaches
and picks it

out
of its loop
like

an apple
from a branch,
the first of the season.

Wintering Out

To board six months
at your mother's place, pay
precious little rent
and not lift a finger, don't think
for a minute I'm moaning.

It's a doll's house end terrace
with all the trimmings: hanging baskets,
a double garage,
a rambling garden with
a fairy-tale ending and geese

on the river. Inside
it's odd, dovetailed into next door
with the bedrooms
back-to-back, wallpaper walls
so their phone calls ring out

loud and clear
and their footsteps on the stairs
run up and down like the practice scales
of a Grade 1 cornet lesson:
their daughter's. From day one

I've been wondering, from the morning
I hoisted the blind
and found
your mother on the lawn
in a housecoat and leggings

expertly skewering fallen fruit
with the outside tine
of the garden fork,
then casting it off, overboard
into the river. I've said

nothing, held my breath
for a whole season, waited
like Johnny Weissmuller
under the ice, held on
to surface in a new house, our own

where the wood
will be treated and buffed and the grain
will circle like weather
round the knots
of high pressure. Here

we've had to button it: not fly
off the handle or stomp upstairs
yelling *That's it you bastard*
and sulk for a week
over nothing. Here

the signs are against us:
some fluke
in the spring water
turning your golden hair lime-green, honey.
Even the expert

from Yorkshire Water
taking pH tests
and fur from the kettle
can't put his finger on it.
We'll have to go; leave

the bathroom with
no lock, the door that opens
of its own accord, the frostless glass
and pretty curtains
that will not meet.

It only takes one night,
your mother
having one of her moments, out
at midnight
undercoating the gutter to catch us

in the bath, fooling around
in Cinemascope. Nothing for it but to dip
beneath the bubbles,
take turns to breathe through the tube
of the loofah, sit tight

and wait for summer.

Two at the End of Winter

I. MARCH 20TH

The path leads onto a Roman road
Skewbald with the old snow and sandstone puddles;
Otherwise the basic winter colours still apply:
Grey, black, occasional green and white.

A cat on the golf course sits and watches
As the smoke keeps curling from the clubhouse
To the hillside where the line of the snow breaks
Occasional green, grey, white and black.

Sheep, looking for patches of thawed ground,
Look themselves like patches of thawed ground
Nosing around in the snow and the trees,
Black, white, grey and occasional green.

Tufted here, threadbare over there, the nap
Of the old bowling green is patched
With poor soil and snow, with water and grass,
White, black, occasional green and grey.

At Laggan House a petrol tank has leaked
Across the wet road. I walk straight through it
Planting rainbow footprints with each step:
Indigo, violet, occasional green and red.

2. HERON

You pull onto the soft verge
And the tyres slacken into the dirt.

I pass the field-glasses
From the glove compartment
And you fumble, finding a focus
Through the action of the wipers

And describe it to me: how it
Hangs in the shallows, shaking the rain
From its featherings. How it watches,
Then cautiously adopts

Its fishing position, then wades
Thoughtfully forward, then holds again.
You go on piecing out the picture
And I affect not to listen

Until you put the glasses down
And I realise you've stopped talking.
We sit there, breathing, steaming up
The windows and watching

As the heron feints
To a fleck on the line of the lake
Like a wood-chip flaw
On slate Ingres paper

And the hilltops are water-marked
If we look hard enough.

Snow Joke

Heard the one about the guy from Heaton Mersey?
Wife at home, lover in Hyde, mistress
in Newton-le-Willows and two pretty girls
in the top grade at Werneth prep. Well,

he was late and he had a good car so he snubbed
the police warning-light and tried to finesse
the last six miles of moorland blizzard,
and the story goes he was stuck within minutes.

So he sat there thinking about life and things;
what the dog does when it catches its tail
and about the snake that ate itself to death.
And he watched the windscreen filling up

with snow, and it felt good, and the whisky
from his hip-flask was warm and smooth.
And of course, there isn't a punchline
but the ending goes something like this:

they found him slumped against the steering wheel
with VOLVO printed backwards in his frozen brow.
And they fought in the pub over hot toddies
as to who was to take the most credit.

Him who took the aerial to be a hawthorn twig?
Him who figured out the contour of his car?
Or him who said he heard the horn, moaning
softly like an alarm clock under an eiderdown?

It Ain't What You Do It's What It Does to You

I have not bummed across America
with only a dollar to spare, one pair
of busted Levi's and a bowie knife.
I have lived with thieves in Manchester.

I have not padded through the Taj Mahal,
barefoot, listening to the space between
each footfall picking up and putting down
its print against the marble floor. But I

skimmed flat stones across Black Moss on a day
so still I could hear each set of ripples
as they crossed. I felt each stone's momentum
spend itself against the water; then sink.

I have not toyed with a parachute chord
while perched on the lip of a light aircraft;
but I held the wobbly head of a boy
at the day centre, and stroked his fat hands.

And I guess that the tightness in the throat
and the tiny cascading sensation
somewhere inside us are both part of that
sense of something else. That feeling, I mean.

Ice

As if the window that will not close
and the bathwater being barely hot enough
and the wet towels
were not enough to worry over.

But your favourite dress
is damp and unironed;
you haven't a stitch to wear
and I am to blame.

Now you will turn the house inside out.
Now you will tear through the wardrobe –
more shoes than Mrs Marcos, hangers
relieved of their shirts and blouses

till the armchair is constricted
with fabrics and colours
and the carpet alive
with cuffs, sleeves and collars.

I wait outside
by the fractured pipe
on the gable end
as the cream of your bathwater

finds its way along the street
and turns the corner.
Already its edges
are beginning to harden.

Zoom!

It begins as a house, an end terrace
in this case
   but it will not stop there. Soon it is
an avenue
   which cambers arrogantly past the Mechanics' Institute,
turns left
   at the main road without even looking
and quickly it is
   a town with all four major clearing banks,
a daily paper
   and a football team pushing for promotion.

On it goes, oblivious to the Planning Acts,
the green belts,
   and before we know it it is out of our hands:
city, nation,
   hemisphere, universe, hammering out in all directions
until suddenly,
   mercifully, it is drawn aside through the eye
of a black hole
   and bulleted into a neighbouring galaxy, emerging
smaller and smoother
   than a billiard ball but weighing more than Saturn.

People stop me in the street, badger me
in the check-out queue
   and ask 'What is this, this that is so small
and so very smooth
   but whose mass is greater than the ringed planet?'
It's just words
   I assure them. But they will not have it.

[45]

★

Mother, any distance greater than a single span
requires a second pair of hands.
You come to help me measure windows, pelmets, doors,
the acres of the walls, the prairies of the floors.

You at the zero end, me with the spool of tape, recording
length, reporting metres, centimetres back to base,
    then leaving
up the stairs, the line still feeding out, unreeling
years between us. Anchor. Kite.

I space-walk through the empty bedrooms, climb
the ladder to the loft, to breaking point, where something
has to give;
two floors below, your fingertips still pinch
the last one-hundredth of an inch . . . I reach
towards a hatch that opens on an endless sky
to fall or fly.

The Ram

Half-dead, hit by a car, the whole of its form
a jiggle of nerves, like a fish on a lawn.
To help finish it off, he asked me to stand
on its throat, as a friend might ask a friend

to hold, with a finger, the twist of a knot.
Then he lifted its head, wheeled it about
by the ammonite, spirograph shells of its horns
till its eyes, on stalks, looked back at its bones.

A Few Don'ts about Decoration

Don't mope. Like Rome
it will not be built in a day,
unlike those raised barns
or Kingdom Halls we've heard of
with their pools of labour,

the elders checking
each side of the plumb-line,
the daughters and their pitchers of milk, full
beyond the brim. Their footings
are sunk before breakfast,

by sundown the last stone
is dressed and laid.
Don't let's kid ourselves, we know less
about third-degree burns
than we did about blowlamps. Don't forget:

it's three of sand to one of cement,
butter the tile and not the wall,
half a pound of spilt nails
will sweep clean with a magnet, soot
keeps coming and coming, sandpaper

smells like money.
Don't do that when I'm painting.
Don't begin anything
with one imperial spanner and a saw so blunt
we could ride bare-arse to London on it.

Also, when you hold down
that square yard of beech
and your eyes widen and knuckles whiten
as the shark's fin of the jigsaw blade
creeps inland . . .

don't move a muscle.
And don't you believe it: those stepladders
are not an heirloom but a death trap;
they will snap tight
like crocodile teeth with me on top

and a poor swimmer. Don't turn up
with till rolls like stair carpets. Don't blame me
if the tiles backflip from the wall
or the shower-head swallow-dives into the tub
and cracks it.

Don't give up hope
till the week arrives when *it's done*,
the corner turned, its back
broken, and everything comes on
in leaps and bounds

that even Bob Beamon would be proud of.
OK, that's a light year away
but like a mountain – it's there.
Don't look down.
Don't say it.

To Poverty

after Laycock

You are near again, and have been there
or thereabouts for years. Pull up a chair.
I'd know that shadow anywhere, that silhouette
without a face, that shape. Well, be my guest.
We'll live like sidekicks – hip to hip,
like Siamese twins, joined at the pocket.

I've tried too long to see the back of you.
Last winter when you came down with the flu
I should have split, cut loose, but
let you pass the buck, the bug. Bad blood.
It's cold again; come closer to the fire, the light,
and let me make you out.

How have you hurt me, let me count the ways:
the months of Sundays
when you left me in the damp, the dark,
the red, or down and out, or out of work.
The weeks on end of bread without butter,
bed without supper.

That time I fell through Schofield's shed
and broke both legs,
and Schofield couldn't spare to split
one stick of furniture to make a splint.
Thirteen weeks I sat there till they set.
What can the poor do but wait? And wait.

How come you're struck with me? Go see the Queen,
lean on the doctor or the dean,
breathe on the major,
squeeze the mason or the manager,
go down to London, find a novelist at least
to bother with, to bleed, to leech.

On second thoughts, stay put.
A person needs to get a person close enough
to stab him in the back.
Robert Frost said that. Besides,
I'd rather keep you in the corner of my eye
than wait for you to join me side by side
at every turn, on every street, in every town.
Sit down. I said sit down.

Indus

for Jonathan and Laurie

Sharks patrol for fingers and toes, under the bottom bunk.
A man with a beard waits in the wardrobe in a long coat.
A boxing-glove face squashes against the glass – don't look.
But up above, the Indian Chief beds down in the skyline:

features quarried from stone, head-dress a dry-stone wall.
And his second sight is a shallow tarn, and his mind's eye
is a ten-pence moon, still rising, and his sixth sense
lifts with the four geese that circle his own horizon.

The Water Snake

We sat on the green bank at the side of the road,
passing the time with the girl who wanted to top herself
but somehow managed to stop herself
from driving her mother's car into the stream below.

The cops were called on a mobile phone, and came,
but not before the village fire brigade, eight men
with cartoon bodies and animal heads, hell-bent
on doing something useless with the hose, the hose

which had, as they say, a mind of its own. Alive,
and way too strong for the one with the donkey's face
    to hold,
it stood up straight, spun round, and spat at the girl,
the girl who wanted to die but was too wet now and
    too cold.

The Centaur

In a dream, climbing the path towards Hill Farm
I count the steps – railway sleepers set into the bank,
holding the earth back. In the stable I hear
the flick of a tail, hooves on a concrete floor.

I crash a topstone through the frozen water trough
and dredge the ice. Then walk, unbolt the door,
and raise the bucket of smoke and broken glass
into the warm, dark space, up to your human face.

The Phoenix

Tvillage cuckoo wer caught one spring
to trap tgood weather, an kept in a tower baht roof.
Tnext mornin tbird'd sprung; tMarsdeners reckoned
ttower wernt builded igh enuff. A ladder wer fetched

to bring tbird dahn, but nubdy'd clahm.
Trust, tha sees. Tladder maht walk. Chap maht be stuck
in clahdcuckooland till Kingdomcumsdy, Godknowswensdy.
Meanwahl, tbird wer nested in Crahther's chimney.

The Mariner's Compass

Living alone, I'm sailing the world
single-handed in a rented house.
Last week I rounded the Cape of Good Hope,
came through in one piece;

this morning, flying fish
lying dead in the porch with the post.
I peg out duvet covers and sheets
to save fuel when the wind blows,

tune the engine so it purrs all night
like a fridge, run upstairs
with the old-fashioned thought
of plotting a course by the stars.

Friends wave from the cliffs,
talk nervously from the coastguard station.
Under the rules, close contact
with another soul means disqualification.

White Christmas

For once it is a white Christmas,
so white the roads are impassable
and my wife is snowbound
in a town untroubled by tractor or snowplough.
In bed, awake, alone. She calls

and we pass on our presents by telephone.
Mine is a watch, the very one
I would have chosen. Hers is a song,
the one with the line *Here come the hills of time*,
and it sits in its sleeve,

unsung and unopened. But the dog downstairs
is worrying, gnawing, howling,
so I walk her through clean snow
along the towpath to the boathouse at a steady pace,
then to my parents' place

where my mother is Marie Curie, in the kitchen
discovering radium, and my father is Fred Flintstone,
and a guest from the past has a look on her face meaning
lie and I'll have your teeth for a necklace, boy,
your eyeballs for earrings,

your bullshit for breakfast,
and my two-year-old niece is baby Jesus,
passing between us with the fruit of the earth
and the light of the world – Christingle – a blood orange
spiked with a burning candle.

We eat, but the dog begs at the table,
drinks from the toilet, sings in the cellar.
Only baby Jesus wanders with me down the stairs
with a shank of meat to see her, to feed her.
Later, when I stand to leave

my father wants to shake me by the hand
but my arms are heavy, made of a base metal,
and the dog wants to take me down the black lane, back
to an empty house again. A car goes by
with my sister inside

and to wave goodnight
she lifts the arm of the sleeping infant Christ,
but I turn my wrist to notice the time. There and then
I'm the man in the joke, the man in a world of friends
where all the clocks are stopped,

synchronising his own watch.

The Two of Us

after Laycock

You sat sitting in your country seat
with maidens, servants waiting hand and foot.
You eating swan, crustaceans, starters, seconds, sweet.
You dressed for dinner, worsted, made to measure. Cut:
me darning socks, me lodging at the gate,
me stewing turnips, beet, one spud,
a badger bone. Turf squealing in the grate –
no coal, no wood.

No good. You in your splendour: leather,
rhinestone, ermine, snakeskin, satin, silk,
a felt hat finished with a dodo feather.
Someone's seen you swimming lengths in gold-top milk.
Me parched, me in a donkey jacket,
brewing tea from sawdust mashed in cuckoo spit,
me waiting for the peaks to melt, the rain to racket
on the metal roof, the sky to split,

and you on-stream, piped-up, plugged-in, you worth a mint
and tighter than a turtle's snatch.
Me making light of making do with peat and flint
for heat, a glow-worm for a reading lamp. No match.
The valleys where the game is, where the maize is –
yours. I've got this plot just six foot long
by three foot wide, for greens for now, for daisies
when I'm dead and gone.

You've got the lot, the full set:
chopper, Roller, horse-drawn carriage, microlight, skidoo,
a rosewood yacht, a private jet.
I'm all for saying that you're fucking loaded, you.
And me, I clomp about on foot from field to street;
these clogs I'm shod with, held together now with segs
and fashioned for my father's father's father's feet –
they're on their last legs.

Some in the village reckon we're alike, akin:
same neck, same chin. Up close that's what they've found,
some sameness in the skin,
or else they've tapped me on the back and you've
        turned round.
Same seed, they say, same shoot,
like I'm some cutting taken from the tree,
like I'm some twig related to the root.
But I can't see it, me.

So when it comes to nailing down the lid
if I were you I wouldn't go with nothing.
Pick some goods and chattels, bits and bobs, like
        Tutankhamen did,
and have them planted in the coffin.
Opera glasses, fob-watch, fountain pen, a case of
        fishing flies,
a silver name-tag necklace full-stopped with a
        precious stone,
a pair of one-pound coins to plug the eyes,
a credit card, a mobile phone,

some sentimental piece of earthenware,
a collar stud, a cufflink and a tiepin,
thirteen things to stand the wear and tear
of seasons underground, and I'll take what I'm standing
    up in.
That way, on the day they dig us out
they'll know that you were something really fucking fine
and I was nowt.
Keep that in mind,

because the worm won't know your make of bone
    from mine.

After the Hurricane

Some storm that was, to shoulder-charge the wall
in my old man's backyard and knock it flat.
But the greenhouse is sound, that chapel of glass
we glazed one morning. We glazed *with* morning.
And so is the hut. And so is the shed.

We sit in the ruins and drink. He smokes.
Back when, we would have built that wall again.
But today it's enough to drink and smoke
amongst mortar and bricks, here at the empire's end.

Leaves on the Line

In the past he was coming by steam and coal,
by breath of water, flame of stone;
we waited for hours then buggered off home.

> Till Leaf Man come
> how long, how long?

At present he comes by diesel or spark;
with an ear to the rail we can hear him talk.
We wait all day then die in the dark.

> How sung, how sung
> the Leaf Man song?

Tomorrow he'll come on a beam of light,
rise like morning, end this wait,
but the rooster croaked and he's already late.

> Till Leaf Man come, how long, how long,
> how sung, how sung the Leaf Man song?

Ara

Joseph of Joshua and Mary Firth; in ye body of ye Chapel.
Sarah the Wife of John Whiteley of Darker; in ye Chancel.
Hannah of Whitelee, who was killed by a heifer.
Betty of James Schofield, of Puleside, drowned with
    ye others.

Abraham Woodhead, Town, who was killed by a cart.
William Walker, High Gate, who cut his own throat.
John Whiteley, of Buckleyhill, who was drowned in
    the Look.
John Marsden, in Mr Haigh's Factory, who was
    accidentally shot.

James Kershaw, Carpenter, by the Fall of a Tree at
    Ashton Binn.
Thomas Hirst of Binn, who was killed in a stonepit.
Joseph Kay of Gatehead, drowned when going for
    the doctor.
Mary, D. of the Rev. Lancelot and Mary Bellas –
    in the Altar.

On Marsden Moor

Above the tree line and below the fog
I watched two men on the opposite slope
hauling wooden poles and slabs of dressed stone
from the foot of the hill towards the top.

They didn't stall – just lifted, carried, dropped.
I watched for an hour or thereabouts,
way off, but close enough in a straight line
to bundle them over with a big shout.

Away from the five o'clock of the town,
out from under the axles and bruised skies
it bothered me that men should hike this far
to hoick timber and rock up a steep bank.

Because what if those poles were fencing posts
to hammer home, divide a plot of land
between the two of them, and those dumb stones
the first steps to a new Jerusalem?

Evening

You're twelve. Thirteen at most.
You're leaving the house by the back door.
There's still time. You've promised
not to be long, not to go far.

One day you'll learn the names of the trees.
You fork left under the ridge,
pick up the bridleway between two streams.
Here is Wool Clough. Here is Royd Edge.

The peak still lit by sun. But
evening. Evening overtakes you up the slope.
Dusk walks its fingers up the knuckles of your spine.
Turn on your heel. Back home

your child sleeps in her bed, too big for a cot.
Your wife makes and mends under the light.
You're sorry. You thought
it was early. How did it get so late?

The Spelling

I left a spelling at my father's house
written in small coins on his front step.
It said which star I was heading for next,
which channel to watch, which button to press.
I should have waited, given that spelling
a voice, but I was handsome and late.

While I was gone he replied with pebbles
and leaves at my gate. But a storm got up
from the west, sluicing all meaning and shape.

I keep his broken spelling in a tin,
tip it out on the cellar floor, hoping
a letter or even a word might form.
And I am all grief, staring through black space
to meet his eyes, trying to read his face.

Fisherwood

There's no reply. I am too late.
But every son carries a key

on a string, noosed around his neck.
I'll let myself in and I'll wait.

So did you just leave? Because here
on the arm of the chair there's heat –

the warm hob left by a hot drink . . .
No, just the sun, the fingerprint

of our nearest star, reaching this far.
I'll sit for a while and I'll weep;

under my eyelids, northern lights
and solar flares shimmer and rage.

Bringing It All Back Home

I was doing what we've all done at some point in our lives,
let's face it, googling my own name, when I dropped
across a website promoting the Cuckoo Day Festival in the
village where I was born and grew up. Attractions included
the Crowning of the Turnip King, the Dead Fish Throwing
Competition, Worm Charming on the bowling green, an
Armed Manhunt across the moor in pursuit of a well-known
car thief, the Wheelbarrow Parade, and the opportunity
to pelt a Tory councillor with out-of-date meat products.
But the event which really caught my eye was the Simon
Armitage Trail, a guided tour which promised to take in
'every nook and cranny of the poet's youth'. I went
straight down to the local joke shop and bought myself a
false wig-and-beard combination, completed the disguise
with a large overcoat, and on the day of the tour made my
way to the old lych gate at the appointed hour.

The turnout was woundingly low: two elderly ladies, three
day trippers who'd missed the coach to Malham Cove, and
some goofy-looking student with a notepad and pen in his
hand. Our guide for the day was wearing a safari outfit,
including khaki shorts and a bullwhip tucked in his belt.
'My name's Bob and thank you for coming,' said Bob,
reading from his notes. 'And it's not just for convenience
that we rendezvous beneath the eaves of this churchyard
building. For it was here, acting as a pallbearer at his great-
grandfather's funeral, that Armitage felt the weight of the
coffin biting into his shoulder, and whose pain and
subsequent tears were mistaken for grief by other
mourners, an experience recounted in his first ever

published poem, "The Black Lie".' The goofy student said, 'That explains the uncertainty of tone in that poem, the sense of loss which is actually an expression of guilt.' 'Exactly,' said Bob. One of the day trippers raised his hand and said, 'Can you tell me how long this is going to take? We thought we might try to catch the ferret juggling at midday.' 'Not long,' said Bob, 'it's not like we're talking Samuel Laycock here, right?' Adopting what I hoped was a Russian accent I cleared my throat and said, 'Are you sure about the lych gate story? Armitage could only have been a toddler when that funeral took place.' Bob said, 'Look, pal, don't start splitting hairs today, all right? I'm only standing in for my wife. When it comes to Simon Armitage she really knows her onions, but her brother's gone down with the shingles – big scabs right around his middle like a boxer's belt – so she's playing Florence Nightingale in Market Harborough while muggins here is left holding the baby. So don't shoot the messenger. I was supposed to be supervising the Bouncy Castle. Anyway, where do you come from?' 'Moscow,' I said, then added, 'Actually a small town about twenty miles to the east,' intending to give the falsehood a kind of detailed veracity. Bob said, 'OK, folks, if Leonid Brezhnev here hasn't got any more questions, let's move on.'

We walked up to the stagnant canal, where, according to Bob, my pet Yorkshire terrier had drowned while retrieving a tennis ball. Bob said, 'Armitage never got over that dog, and the whole sorry incident is recorded in his sonnet "Man's Best Friend". Who knows, maybe he should have gone in himself instead of sending that poor mutt to its death.' 'Presumably that explains some of the emotional retardation in his later work,' said the goofy student, whose front teeth were getting longer by the minute. 'Exactly,' said Bob. We waited for one of the day trippers, who'd wandered off along the towpath to read a noticeboard about horse-drawn barges in the nineteenth century, then the tour continued. With Bob spouting his stuff at every lamp post, we walked to a dilapidated cowshed where I was gored by a bull when I was nine, supposedly, then to the escarpment where I'd seen my father bring down a fieldfare with a single stone. Then to Bunny Wood where I'd found Gossip John hanging by the neck, then to a meadow where I'd fallen asleep and woken up with a grass snake curled on my chest, then behind the undertaker's parlour, where, Bob confidently announced, I'd lost my virginity to a girl called Keith. The two ladies tittered behind their hands. We wandered in a big circle for a couple of hours before arriving in the park, and congregated around the bronze, life-size statue of Simon Armitage. 'Of course it caused a huge stink at the time,' said Bob, lighting a cigarette and tossing the spent match into the bandstand. 'It looks like something to be proud of,' I said, from behind my beard. Bob rounded on me: 'Oh really? Well maybe that's how it looks from the Kremlin, but as it happens a lot of people in this village said the money should have gone to the Children's Hospice instead. Those kids with their big eyes and shaved heads – breaks your heart. But don't ask me, I'm only a taxpayer.' Goofy said, 'And once Armitage had packed his bags for Los Angeles he never came back.' 'Exactly so, son, exactly so,' said Bob. Then with the tip of his cigarette he pointed towards the white splodge on Armitage's scalp and the white streaks on his metal face and said, 'But at least the seagulls like it.' And everyone laughed. Bob said, 'All right, people, that just about wraps it up.' 'But what about the house, the Simon Armitage Homestead Experience?' I wanted to know. Bob sighed, impatiently. 'OK, Boris, take the keys and post them back through the letterbox when you're done. It's the one at the top of the hill with the broken windows. There's a compulsory donation of five pounds and be sure to wear the plastic overshoes. And don't touch a thing – it's just as he left it.' I said, 'You mean with the tin of mustard powder on the kitchen table, and a line of his father's ironed shirts hanging from the picture rail, the fancy ones that he wore on stage? And a folded newspaper propped on the arm of the chair, the cryptic crossword laddered with blue ink? And his mother's reading glasses, one arm folded the other outstretched, next to the silver pen?' Bob said, 'You tell me, you're the expert, Mr First Monkey in Space. Now, if you don't mind, I want to see Martin Amis opening the Duck Race, and we're running late.'

Harmonium

The *Farrand Chapelette* was gathering dust
in the shadowy porch of Marsden Church
and was due to be bundled off to the tip
or was mine, for a song, if I wanted it.

Sunlight through stained glass which on bright days
might beatify saints or raise the dead
had aged the harmonium's softwood case
and yellowed the fingernails of its keys,
and one of its notes had lost its tongue
and holes were worn in both the treadles
where the organist's feet in grey woollen socks
and leather-soled shoes had pedalled and pedalled.

But its hummed harmonics still struck a chord:
it had stood facing the choristers' stalls
where father then son had opened their throats
and gilded finches – like high notes – had streamed out.

Through his own blue cloud of tobacco smog,
with smoker's fingers and dottled thumbs,
he comes to help me cart it away.
We lay it flat then carry it out on its back,
and him being him he has to say
that the next box I'll shoulder through this nave
will bear the load of his own dead weight.
And me being me I mouth in reply
some shallow or sorry phrase or word
too starved of breath to make itself heard.

Emergency

The four-pump petrol garage
finally closed,
its defeated owner
inhaling his ghost
in a disused quarry
by coupling the lips of his car exhaust
to the roots of his lungs
via a garden hose.

On the bulldozed forecourt
they threw up a tram shed
for decommissioned emergency vehicles
where a skeleton workforce
service all manneration
of mothballed workhorses
for occasional call-outs
to sitcoms, period dramas and film sets.

And the actual fire station
is up for rent,
that chapel-shaped building
where they stabled the one engine,
spit-buffing and wire-woolling
the chrome fenders,
T-Cutting the steel coachwork
to a flame red;

so what you see,
as the letting agent puts it,
is what you get:
boot cupboard, functional kitchenette,
brass hooks – two still holding
a brace of yolk-yellow plastic helmets –
northlight roof windows
and inspection pit.

The makeshift crew
were volunteer part-timers:
butchers, out-menders,
greasy perchers and hill farmers,
who'd pitch up in bloody aprons,
boiler suits or pyjamas
then venture forth,
fire-slaying on the tender,

and sometimes in dreams
my fire-fighting forefathers
appear, cosmonaut-like,
breathing from oxygen cylinders
through a sudden parting
of towering black cumulonimbus
on fully telescoped
turntable ladders.

The bank's gone as well,
and also the post office,
though in the store-cum-off-licence
you can sign a gyro
with a string-and-sellotape-tethered
half-chewed biro
or deface a scratchcard
or sell a bullmastiff.

The horizon ablaze –
is it moor-fire or sundown?
In the local taproom
prescription jellies and tin-foil wraps
change hands under cover
of *Loot* magazine
and Tetley beer mats.
What is it we do now?

October

All day trimming branches and leaves, the homeowner
sweeping the summer into a green heap;
all evening minding the flames,
inhaling the incense of smouldering laurel and pine.

Or careering home from school down Dog Shit Lane
between graves and allotments,
the old churchwarden propped on a rake
in a standing sleep, bent over a fire
of cut flowers and sympathy cards and wreaths.

Snow

The sky has delivered
its blank missive.
The moor in coma.
Snow, like water asleep,
a coded muteness
to baffle all noise,
to stall movement,
still time.
What can it mean
that colourless water
can dream
such depth of white?
We should make the most
of the light.

Stars snag
on its crystal points.
The odd, unnatural pheasant
struts and slides.
Snow, snow, snow
is how the snow speaks,
is how its clean page reads.
Then it wakes, and thaws,
and weeps.

~

can a berth be reserved? |
    this western sector
        not *christened* yet,

ground unbroken, turf intact |
    laced with preservatives
        wooden telegraph poles

embalm the day,
    hoist live power lines
        fizzing in damp air

above hawthorn and dwarf birch |
    a spooked blackbird
        trapezes low

over a mown verge |
    here a body lies
        angled, inclined towards

semaphoring turbine blades
    on Scapegoat Hill
        or the silhouette shack

of the shooting lodge
    under Scout Rock |
        here the skull is aligned,

eye sockets fired
        by moor blaze
                necklacing nabs and crowns

or low red sun
        igniting the fonts
                of Butterley, Blakeley,

Swellands, Cupwith,
        Redbrook, Sparth, Wessenden,
                Wessenden Head,

Deer Hill, March Haig,
        Tunnel End, Black Moss
                and Little Black Moss

~

in the dream again
        he *leadeth* me
                along Shady Row –

that canyoned track
        between teetering mills –
                to tightrope walk

the dye-pan walls |
        and *leadeth* me
                to the shunting yard

and the cinder tips,
        onto Ready Carr
                (you following this?) |

then to Bramhall's field |
        then above Wood Top
                to the sycamore tree

we gouged and stabbed
        (it's been felled)
                by Beardsall's hut |

and *leadeth* me
        to that unnamed tract
                where Old Mount Road

shadows Rock View,
        past the clumps of woodbine
            we tried to smoke |

through abandoned allotments
        and chicken coops,
                over footings and earthworks,

Phoenician hearths,
        Etruscan foundries,
                the palimpsest of Jerusalem

under Yorkshire stone,
        the Marsden cuckoo
                alive in its tomb,

its muffled
        fuck you, fuck you;
                fuck you, fuck you

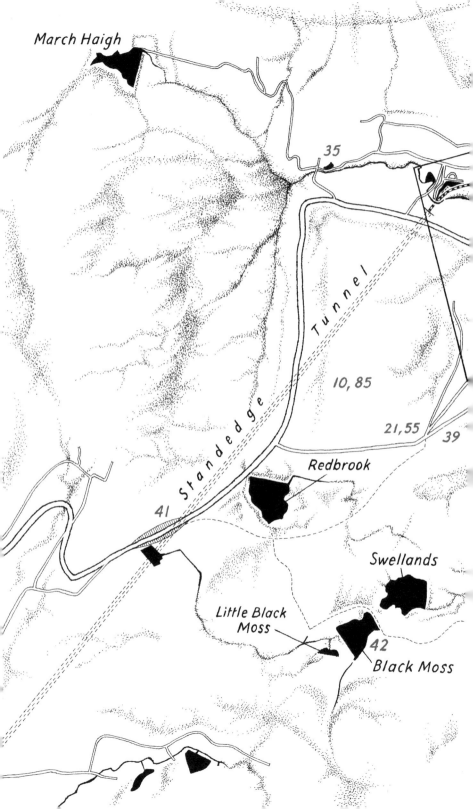